POSTMORTEM SAY

Amanda Newell

Červená Barva Press
Somerville, Massachusetts

Červená Barva Press
P.O. Box 440357
W. Somerville, MA 02144-3222

www.cervenabarvapress.com

Bookstore: www.thelostbookshelf.com

Cover art: by Nancy Mitchell

Cover design: William J. Kelle

ISBN: 978-1-950063-82-6

Library of Congress Control Number: 2024934072

ACKNOWLEDGMENTS

The Baltimore Review, "Because I Am Lonely and You Will Not
    Know My Pain"
Cultural Weekly, "Permanent Girl"
The Cimarron Review, "How to Track a Body," "Portent"
Gargoyle, "Child, Out—," "Elastration," "The Black and White of
    Him in His Wetsuit," "Out of Body," "The Day After the
    Latest Mass Shooting"
North American Review, "Thundering Horse"
Plume, "Ammunition" (formerly "Carry"), "Quotidian" "Meditation
    on a Shower Rod at the Super 8"
Pittsburgh Poetry Review, "Nurse"
Rattle, "Late Sonogram"
Rhino Poetry, "Butchering the Sika Deer"
storySouth, "Leaving Lime Kiln Road," "Deer Madness"
SWWIM, "Meditation on My Right Breast in Stall Number Seven"
The Summerset Review, "First Kill"
Voices from the Attic, "A Woman From the Infant Mortality Review
    Board Calls"
Zone 3, "The Hunter's Wife"

"Because I Am Lonely and You Will Not Know My Pain," was a
winner in *The Baltimore Review's* tools-themed contest, Winter
2019.

"A Woman From the Infant Mortality Review Board Calls" was
selected by Lynn Emanuel as the winning poem for Carlow
University's 2015 Patricia Dobler Poetry Award.

"First Kill" appeared in the chapbook *Fractured Light* (Broadkill
River Press).

~

My heartfelt thanks to everyone at Červená Barva Press, and to
Gloria Mindock, for bringing this book into the world. I'm
honored to be part of the Červená Barva family.
I'm tremendously grateful to Sue Ellen Thompson, Nancy Mitchell,
Robin Rosen Chang, and Dan O'Brien for their friendship and

careful reading of my manuscript. My gratitude to Peter Campion for "what happens when we talk." Thanks also to Nancy Robson, Sarah Everdell, Meredith Davies Hadaway, JoAnn Balingit, Ellen Wise, Erin Murphy, Leeya Mehta, Michael Glaser, Danny Lawless, Richard Peabody, and John Elsberg—all friends in craft, all of whom have inspired and encouraged me across the years.

Thank you to Nancy Mitchell for the extraordinary cover art.

I'm grateful as well to The MFA Program for Writers at Warren Wilson College and to Ellen Bryant Voigt and Debra Allbery for their leadership and vision. Special thanks to my advisors Alan Shapiro, Martha Rhodes, Daisy Fried, and Connie Voisine for their extraordinary mentorship. I'd be remiss not to acknowledge others in the Warren Wilson community who provided critical feedback on many of the poems here: Susan Jo Russell, Trish Marshall, Mark Elber, Shannon Winston, Leigh Lucas, and Cecille Marcato. And for their ongoing fellowship, I extend my gratitude to Nicole Chvatal, Jill Klein, Annabella Johnson, Nomi Stone, Rose Skelton, Jodie Free, Shannon Castleton, Dan Jenkins, and Amanda Shaw.

And, of course, my deepest gratitude goes to my beloveds: Jake, Ben, and my entire family, without whom this book would not have been possible. I love you.

TABLE OF CONTENTS

About the Author

POSTMORTEM SAY

Ammunition

After Fang snapped photos of the boys & sent them to you
to show he knew where we lived & where they went to daycare,

your carry permit came in two days & so did the state police,
who drove from Pikesville to surveil our home the way you

surveil with trail cams the deer you hunt with your bow
& muzzleloader, the 12 gauge that leans against the safe

in the game room, where you keep all your dead.
Your .45 caliber Sig Sauer is the thing you said

would keep us safe, that you still keep loaded, no safety,
in your jeans drawer. Because a gun is no good

if you can't get to it in time. Because a good man
with a gun is better than. Because the worst part of a threat is

the always-waiting-but-never-knowing-when of it.
Sometimes I dream I die at the Food Lion—close range,

a single shot to the head, my blood spattering frozen
peas & lima beans. Sometimes I dream you die,

your body bagged, loaded on a stretcher outside the county
courthouse. I have learned to live with drawerfuls of shotshells

& the clink of brass bullets as they spill from your pockets
in the spin cycle. I have learned the hollow-point bullet

is best for self-defense because of the way it blooms
in soft tissue. But the day you left your Sig, loaded,

on the kitchen table, the boys were home, & I learned
I could say it: "I will leave you." How many times

have I sworn it? "Don't make promises you can't keep,"
Chekhov said. "One must not put a loaded rifle on the stage

if no one is thinking of firing it." Yet, here we are,
loaded guns across the page, & I still can't pull the trigger.

~

Child, Out—

       Didn't want him
             sliding through the strange blue,   stall

flung open,   tits dripping—   Not another child
lost,   ashes   for the letter block.

          O, where is my shoe? you cried   & were happy
to be paralyzed.

       Are we too yellow? Too thin?
             Pleasegodnocolic.

Quick!
Say *hello hello*

       to your ophthalmologist,   Dr. Z
       & smile—

            How embarrassing to be seen
                like this. He's operating,

but not on you.   Enter Nurse D
         in recovery.   Her son's thirty now & divorced,

         so sad. Good thing she knows
            how to tend a wound.   Towel

after soaking towel of it,
of you—
           she's cleaning the blood, post-

un-gutting,   the putting-back-together again.

The Hunter's Wife

He strung deer
from trees, flayed
muskrats on the porch,

and picked ducks
in the sink, leaving
the guts for her to scrape.

"There is no waste,"
he'd say. But for her,
it was always the taste—

too wild, too raw
to stomach. She'd turn
away from the plate.

Deer Madness

They're out there now,
        careening across frost-
hard fields, springing
        onto roads like Olympic
gymnasts—so many
        accidents waiting.

On my way to you tonight,
        I watch for the brown
sliver skimming pines,
        the white tuft of flicking
tail in twilight. It's the peak
        of the rut, when a doe

will sometimes abandon
        her young to breed again.
I envy that freedom,
        the no-thought-
to-consequences-of it.
        But "selfish" is what I said

the day my neighbor sent
        her girls to school,
then left for Texas with her lover.
        No one suspected,
least of all her witless
        husband. Still, the signs

had been there: her sudden
        weight loss (desire thins),
her new job (mere pretext).
        And her children?
I can't stand looking at them
        anymore, their moon-blank

faces at the bus stop.
        What could they know
of the body, how it goes

where it must, like the doe
who's running into
　　　my lights? I can see it now

in the wet glint of her
　　　dark eye—that wild hunger—
before she's gone
　　　so quickly I wonder
if I've seen her at all.
　　　Or if anything can stop her.

How to Track a Body

You can track a body
by the blood
it leaves. You will
need patience.
You may need
to get on your hands
and knees and
crawl through brown
stalk and winter
thicket. You may
find yourself
walking in circles
for hours when
the trail goes cold.
You may never
find it. You may
need to come back
the next day and
look again in the light.
You will need
a good eye to see
threads of white
snagging briars,
to tell one kind
of blood from another,
gut from liver,
lung from heart.
A lung shot,
for instance, foams
pink, but a heart
shot is darker.
It spills all at once.

First Kill

Our son shoots a deer
during muzzleloader season—
a doe, small enough to fit into the cooler
my husband brought with him.
The picture is already on the computer screen:
our boy, smiling as he kneels
over his kill, her blood staining
the leaves. One day,
there will be another body
spread before him. She, too, will bleed.

A Woman From the Infant Mortality Review Board Calls

No, I am not an addict.
Yes, I had a doctor.
No, we are not smokers.
No, I do not want you
coming to our home.

I could see it
on the sonogram's
chalk sketch, the club-
foot and cleft palate,
fingers like vines.
Some extra ones.
"A one-in-ten-thousand
error of cell division,"
the specialist said.
"Most women
miscarry before it gets
this far."

Thirty hours
after the pitocin
and morphine,
after the resident
shoved his gloved
fist into me
to ripen my cervix
with a kelp stick,
I gave birth
to a shiny bruised
doll—small enough
to fit into a wicker
Easter basket—
whose silence
was welcome.

Out of Body

All night, cobalt
skies and purple
dandelions. Many
red balloons.
The ones who lived—

so far—are safe,
tubed and sleeping
in their plastic
cubes. Why not
mine? Here,

nothing but needles
and deep-sea
tangle. In my hands,
almost-you.

The Black and White of Him in His Wetsuit

Thin, cigarette
loose between
his fingers. It was

the day of Sicily.
Of frogmen
and the Mediterranean.

Of blue tattoos.
Before the Playa
Girón and whole

team gone.
Before blasted spine
and barely alive.

Before *go to hell*
on checks sent
back to the government.

If I had known him
then, had even been born.

Portent

He'd gone again,
dressed in camo
and a bullet-proof
vest, Sig at his hip.
Gone despite her
constant nagging,
the why-go-if-you-
don't-have-to and
what-if-something-
happens pleas.
    But where else
the exhilaration?
With their sickly
boys, three and one,
who never slept?
With his depressed,
distant wife, who left
piles of laundry,
never cooked
cleaned
gardened?
Who cut her eyes
at him (yes,
he'd seen her), his
heavy foot,
the shaking floor?
    Still, he always
came home, no
different tonight,
but for the quickly-
conjured summer
storm—his pickup
struck by lightning
as he pulled into
the drive—and he,
nearly burned alive
while she'd been
where? Safe, inside.

And later swore
she hadn't heard him—
"Unlock it,
dammit!"—his
fists on the door.

Leaving Lime Kiln Road

As if I could exchange
my life like shoes

bought a half size
too small, trade

the corn-tasseled
flatness for pines

& limestone,
I said it, "I want

to leave him,"
put my fingers

to your lips, blue
ribbon of my car's

exhaust wavering,
"I want to leave him."

I play & replay
your words until

"I don't want you to"
becomes "I don't want you,"

the crush
of wheels on gravel.

~

Thundering Horse

1.

He's talking about dying.
We're in his kitchen.
Scarlet the macaw
is shrieking again on her perch.
I've already written
my obituary, he says.
It will be one sentence:
"He was a Tuscarora Indian."

I take a sip of wine.
You can't control what people write about you,
I say, when you're dead.
Oh yes, he says, I can.

2.

Like a wife, I keep a list of his habits:
He prefers wearing white polos.
He sneezes five times
and always after sex. He smokes
Gispert Toro,
shops in bulk at Costco.
On Saturdays, he tunes nitrous-blown
racing engines on the black and white
checkerboard floor of his garage.
It smells like grease and wrenches
and is full of shiny old cars with big wheels
and names like Tin Indian and Dark Horse.
Once, he let me sit in the front seat of Swindler A.

3.

saturday i'm busy and sunday is my poker day,
he wrote in his last email,
not bothering to capitalize or punctuate.
I felt small.

I felt my heart contract. Then I cried
long, wailing tears in my car where no one could see or hear me.
There is nothing I hate more than a spectacle.
I resolved to be done with him.
Who, I asked, pounding the wheel, has more to lose?

4.

I try, but cannot
name the source of my attraction to him.
There is nothing
beautiful about him.
His face is wrinkled,
his knees are swollen.
Why? I ask myself.
The first time we tried to fuck
he said, I have a confession to make.
This morning, I –
Then he went into the other room
and returned with a glass of water and a Viagra.
He said, Give me thirty minutes.
He is older than my father. I know
what people—even my friends—
would say, if they knew.
Well, and so what.
I ask if things would be different
for us if I left.
I've tried to be straight with you, he says.
There is no one else in my life.
I consider this.
Not having another
is different than wanting
another. Does he
want another? I am,
I realize, a convenience.

It is a moment of great clarity.

5.

What I need, he says,
is a dream. A vision that lets me know
it's OK for us.
What have we been doing
if it's not OK?
I ask. Why keep doing it.
And who knows how long it might take
to summon a vision.
It might come
tomorrow. It might
come in a year.
It might never.

He says we have no choice
but to keep traipsing toward the horizon.

6.

I went to a psychic.
Maybe she could be more specific.
She said J. would never let me "walk beside him."
He does care for you, though, she said.
I haven't been back to her since.

7.

The last time I spent the night with him, I dreamed
we were walking through the woods
holding hands.
The forest floor, downy with pine needles,
seemed to be breathing
under our feet, a snake-like undulation of the earth.
Then the dismembered heads
of eagles began to emerge, unburying themselves,
each terrible head pulsing as if to say
Look what you've done.

8.

One-person birds, he says,
Macaws. She's screaming at you
because she's jealous.
She sits on her perch
in the kitchen, chews seeds
and spits them onto the floor.
She likes to interrupt our conversations
when we cook.
Sometimes he throws
a crumpled Coke can at her cage
to quiet her. Or he'll cover her
with a sheet, banish her to the basement.
He says he's already made arrangements
in his will for her.
Lucky bird.

9.

A dreamcatcher with sun-
bleached feathers dangled from the rearview mirror
of his 1985 red Chevy pickup
with the bumper sticker,
Custer Had It Coming.

He parked it on the shoulder of Route 15.
It was early morning,
a wet gray mist over the Blue Ridge
as we traipsed across the field to the burial mound.

I wore a skirt but the field was unmown
and I could feel the sting of briars and weeds
against my legs as we circled the mound,
offering to the earth pinches of tobacco.
For a long time, he stood
in front of an old tree,
face pressed to the bark.
I never asked him what he saw there.
Or whom.

Later, my legs—crosshatched with cuts—swelled so badly
I couldn't walk.

10.

I had ridden in his pickup before,
so many years ago,
when he was married and we drove into town for lunch.
He was wearing his bear claw necklace
and as we passed the redbuds in full bloom,
I thought of how they looked like clouds of cotton candy.
He leaned toward me and said, You know
where this is going, right?

11.

Mostly I wonder when and how he will die.
Who will tell me. I consider giving my number
to his son and asking him to call
when something happens to his father.
It seems like begging.
I may have to beg.
Promise me, I say to J.
Promise me you'll talk to me when you're dead.
It is impossible and it is ridiculous
but still it is my only hope.
You will have to ask, he says.
Who am I to call him back?
I imagine myself at the burial mound,
sitting cross-legged in front of his favorite tree,
offering tobacco, like grief, to the wind.

~

The Big Bear Singers

are loud today on his radio,
Where are you I am here I am here.

Call and response, Sunday morning.
"A couples dance," he says, two-stepping

to the drum of a moccasin dance.
But when the call comes

(*Where are you?*) he wants no drama.
Admit nothing, deny everything—

I hate it. (*I am here I am here.*)
Our relationship is one of no

beginning, no end. He is happy
with his twelve cows and one bull, fifty-

thousand dollars of fencing—a steal
that will last him ten, maybe fifteen

years, what's left of his life. I could be
happy here too—white farmhouse,

weeping willow, red glow of Appalachian
dusk light. (*I am here I am here.*)

"Will you be here?" I ask. "I am not,"
he says, "going anywhere." (*Where are you?*)

Elastration

He banded the bull calves
in the farmhouse kitchen,
then waited for their balls
to drop in the grass or hay.
He said it was more humane.
They were too young
to know pain was pain.

Quotidian

Steak dinners are the worst /you prefer the fatty cut / those white-ribboned slabs from Save-A-Lot / I want something leaner / no red please / at the table you pick the gristle from your teeth / that's Rule #4 / don't pick your teeth at the table / not even with a toothpick / we don't have any toothpicks / I don't keep them in stock / ha / also don't shovel or stab your food / that's #3 & you do that too / you eat like a truck driver is what father would say / don't hunch / do we need to send you to finishing school? / btw he was a lip purser / would wave his fork up & down like a conductor / as though the air at the table were turbulent / how do I disgust you? / he'd spit / mother kept colored toothpicks in the cabinet / I liked the blue & pink ones best / I've watched you now for years / & who knows how many more we've got / I don't math / I wouldn't say you're a lip smacker exactly / more of a lip revver the way they start spinning before the fork / in anticipation of / like you're warming up for the buffet race / it is all so irritating / the sound of your hunger / the taptaptap of silver on ceramic / that popping jaw

Colt

Colt was a one-percenter
a Pagan enforcer and real
mean he could crush
a shot glass between his teeth
he was father's friend
and mostly quiet unless he was
drinking in which case
it was a different story as it was
when he stole the keys
one New Year's Eve and drove
father's Jag into a tree
after which Colt disappeared
with his new arm to Florida
where I hear he's dying now of cancer
don't go asking questions
father warns me not to go
looking for trouble the way I did
when I was seven and ran
downstairs to see who was breaking in
who had tripped the alarm
I'll never forget he smacked me
across the face how it stung
he meant to stop me he said I'm sorry
it's for your own good

Meditation on My Right Breast in Stall Number Seven

How it sags under its own weight,
so much bigger
than the left. Asymmetric.
I take it in my palm.

Shake it a little.
What's inside?
Microcalcifications.
A sack of marbles.

Maybe nothing. Probably
nothing. Still,
there's potential
architectural distortion.

Could be a sign of—
"architectural distortion—
scared," writes
Sarah2158. At sixty,

her breasts should not be
getting thicker.
And Nightcrawler
was just diagnosed

with ductal carcinoma.
Lately, I've been reading
cancer threads
on Reddit. Sometimes

women post updates,
sometimes not.
You can never be sure
who's still alive

by the time you read them.
And the X-rays
of cancerous breasts?
Translucent globes

of streaming white
threads cinched
at the point of malignancy.
Almost beautiful.

I always wanted to be
beautiful. I have always
wanted too much.
If I'm lucky today,

I'm only lucky.
It's frailty that scares me,
the slow rot.
Being spared long enough

to watch while the ones
we love the most
suffer for reasons
they cannot seem to explain.

Permanent Girl

She's fifty now   tired of riding the blue anchor on his left
bicep   tired of being his USNA pinup girl   always fighting

gravity   bubbled tits & ass sagging on the freckled folds
of his skin. The things she's seen!   The pool halls & Sundays

at Hollywood Casino!   Now her legs cramp   she's got
varicose veins   numb fingers & toes   (from clinging   so long

to the shank)   & furthermore   doesn't like what little she can
see in the mirror   her face & mermaid hair a gauzy blur.

Threads of silver sprout from her crotch   they make her itch.
Sometimes she bleeds   leaves flakes on his pillow   & although

she tries to tell him to moisturize   her lips are perennially
puckered.   Still   she's his permanent girl!   No one has

lasted as long.   She knows what he likes   what positions
she's seen the dog-eared pages of *The Complete Guide to Sex*

his drawer of vibrating   blinking cocks   but lately she
wonders what will happen after he dies   whether they'll burn

or be buried together   in which case she will outlive him
& by how many years   who can say

Nurse

Tilting your head back
                    you let me squeeze   each drop into
                                              the bloodshot, milk
                              blue, where I can see
            it, what my life   would be like
                              with you,

parceling pills,
                    wheeling you and   your oxygen tank
                                              around the farm,
                                              your lungs
crumbling—sex,
              by then, the Viagra—out

                                              of the question.

I am afraid of it,
                    fear   you dying
                                          on top of me.
You dying at all.
                              I often wonder how
                              and how soon. I could
                                          do it right now,

in your kitchen with

                    the sharp one you use
                                          for onions, slide it
so gently   across your throat.

How much easier
                    it would be and how
                                          almost painless.

36

Because I Am Lonely and You Will Not Know My Pain

I am pausing you at six seconds,
just after you turn
from the hood of the old
blue Mercury to look back
at the camera, at me,
though I am not there (not yet),
not the one recording
how the wind, as you adjust
the ignition coil, will whip
across your lips the loose
strands of your hair,
or how, beneath your fingers,
the Ironhorse will fire again,
so loudly that everything—
even the camera—will shake
with the force of three thousand horses.

~

Meditation on a Shower Rod at the Super 8

You and I are snakebit. Can we postpone?
Your words, liquid-lit in my palm like a fortune.

I don't know what, exactly, being "snakebit" means
to the Tuscarora, but I know enough to know
we've been poisoned, spiritually speaking.

Maybe this time for good. By whom, I don't yet know.

~

My search results say the water snake is
a Tuscarora legend. Abnormally large,
it rises from the depths of the lake to seize its human prey.

Like the pit viper, who will strike
when threatened, it prefers to be left alone,
which is how I am beginning to think I would like to be left by you.

~

Did you know my ninth grade English teacher was fired
for telling us suicide is the final fuck you?

I'm thinking my thinking about her right now
may have something to do with—let's face it—
how little you must think of me,

and the clarity that comes after five hours of driving
straight through the heart
of Jesus country, where every barn roof and billboard
preaches the Word to the road-weary.
You can save yourself in Bristol. You can repent in Johnson City.

You can stop traffic
at the top of the Bay Bridge and pray

no one will stop you from jumping.

~

When I don't respond:
Did you get my message?

Who is she, I want to ask, but don't, as I scroll through
hundreds of pages of bloated faces, blistered feet, charcoaled flesh.

Thou Shalt Be Saved, said the sign. Is this why
they put Bibles in every bedside drawer—
Thy Rod and Thy Staff, etc.? And why not put my faith
in something real, something I can put my hands on?
Here, in the hot glare of bath light, such a shiny promise.

Foliage

      Your weedy hair gathered
in silver-clasped ponytails.

      Mine, admit it, no silk
      bolt
        of sweet corn.

What was I
  to you?

   Morning?
     the ruby-throated
hummingbirds?

The Customer

He was rushing,
had a plane to catch
back to West Palm
at five, wasn't sure
what shirt size—
the extra small
in winter white?
The extra-extra small?
"She's five feet tall,"
he said, raising
his hand to approximate
her smallness.
"And very athletic—"
I imagined the sleek
calves and compact
quads of a tumbler,
her chalk-dusted
leotard, ripples
of ribs, small
slopes of muscle
where her breasts
should be. No doubt
she was younger.
Much. Maybe
a new second
marriage. What man
shops this way
for a wife of x years?
I watched as he
browsed the sale,
lightly touching
with his fingertips
the ruffled
folds of each
white blouse
before settling
on the extra-extra
small, which lay

across the display
table, his desire
so clearly meant to please
in order to be
pleased. No,
they were lovers,
I guessed.
In the betweenness
of here and there,
flickering shadow
world of being
nowhere-in-
particular, I existed
for him in this
single moment
of transit only
as the ringer
at cash/wrap,
one more stop
on the way to—
So when he asked
if I would please
box the blouse
and the blue
tweed suit
from the other
store, even though
he was sorry,
he knew I was
not supposed to,
I did—
because I could do
this one thing
for him, which was
a small thing,
and because I
wanted just once
again to be
that small—

He, who once gave me

a bear claw   eagle feather   hand-sewn
                                  moccasins—
                                        he, who once

claimed me
                      as his wife,   says
he wants only his solitude
and his cows—

                                    and I, who have never
                                    been ashamed,
                                        am now, finally—

time to go home,
                    but where?

                                    To the unsuspecting one?

Butchering the Sika Deer

Bound by her hind legs,
she dangles from the maple—
so small she twirls a little
in the breeze. I watch my son
as he works the knife slowly
along the split seam of the cow's
belly, peeling away the cotton
flaps of her hide like a sock
until nothing is left but flesh
wrapped in white swirls
of gauzy tissue. I did not teach him
how to call for his prey
on the marsh, how to shoot
a living thing, how to butcher it.
That was his father.
Like his father, he does not mind
the blood. He'll take what he needs,
nothing more. When he's done,
he'll drag what's left
of her into the woods.

All Kinds of Stories

My body will not lie. Every time, within a week.
Back at the urgent care, peeing into a cup, again
my son's friend's mother is working her shift
again like she was the time before and the time
before that. Stress, she says, will do it every time,
and again I do not disagree. Again, I shift
the conversation to our boys. But then again
I have to admit I did not know my son
had spent the night at their house two days
ago. I had not been at home where I sleep
alone, my husband on the couch—his snoring
and a bad foot. At least that's what we tell
ourselves. If there is one thing I have learned:
you can tell yourself anything.
You can tell yourself all kinds of stories.

The Day After the Latest Mass Shooting

He's ready to blow up his calc book
at the firing range, my student.

I almost laugh.

"I need to go shoot something."

I need

to go
shoot

something.

It's funny, right?—

      Hundreds of pages of equations petal-

      fluttering through the powder-singed air.

Perhaps this is what happens
after twenty years on the Chesapeake.

You become accustomed.

      Shotguns, puffy camo,

      straight pipe trucks.

      Confederate-themed everything:

            crab stickers, license plates,
            tattered flags on the front

            lawns of foreclosed homes.

When our son was born,

my husband dressed him

in a camo onesie. I was

still on the table,

bleeding where they cut

& stapled me.

What was it the therapist said
to my son about processing anger?

"Punch a pillow."

"Take a walk."

"Always let your parents know
where you're going."

My son.
Who would never—

Who clung to my leg as a toddler.

Who wrote a poem at ten
called "The Front Yard Cardinal."

Now, he prefers shooting

blackbirds & keeps his

bedroom door closed

while he's killing

virtual enemies.

My son.

Who says he wants an AR-15
when he turns eighteen.

Who knows whether he's joking.

Foreclosure

Missing shingles like lost teeth,
sun-baked shutters.

Always last on the block to mow
after rain, and even then, only

in front. The rest of the yard—
like us—we let go. Yellow jackets

angry-swarm burning bushes.
The dumpster's full.

Late Sonogram

I bled through the first month of every pregnancy.
I have been bleeding for weeks. I am bleeding even now,
and I have ruined at least fifteen pairs of underwear.
Poet M says no one wants to read about my underwear,

especially not in the first stanza. She said nothing
about the second, though, or where in the poem
the poet *should* introduce the subject of her underwear
if she's going to write about it. Poet A didn't mind underwear
in the first stanza. But it was only my first draft,
and maybe he was afraid to say anything.

The nurse draws blood and checks my vitals,
which are mostly normal. I tell her there's not enough
triple-ply on the Eastern Shore to stanch my flow.
That I've cleared the aisles of every store
within fifty miles. I tell her it's unlikely although possible:
I could be pregnant. But at my age, the question of age
begins to sound accusatory. "Are you still using birth control?"
What she really means: at forty-seven, you're too old

to have another baby. Later I tell the doctor, who looks fifteen,
that I have an IED. No. I mean an IUD.
I get them confused all the time,
ever since I started writing poems about my former student,
who nearly died when a bomb was blown up under his foot.
Right now my uterus feels like it is going to explode.

Speaking of explosions.

I took some students to an abortion rally in Annapolis this week.
I couldn't stop staring at the parking garage behind the stage
and all that dark, open space between the pillars,
where anyone could hide with a gun and snipe at us.
I promised their parents we'd be safe.
How can anyone promise that? The ice cream truck

turned anti-abortion-Jesus-mobile that we'd seen earlier

never showed up with its megaphone. I'm not sure,
but I think there was a suspicious and possibly explosive
device in the cemetery and the bomb squad was called
(I heard the sirens).
But no one looked too worried, and we walked right past
the cemetery and police officers on the way back to my car.

Then again, no one in the mall last summer looked all that worried
when the newspaper shooting was happening across the street.
People were still eating outside at California Pizza Kitchen
as the office building was evacuated. I remember it was
a nice day—blue sky, not too hot for the end of June.

I thought about advising my students to scatter and run in zigzags
if anything happened, but I didn't, and nothing awful happened,
and then we ate pancakes, and everyone got home safely.
No blood. Isn't that the barometer these days?

When the boys were toddlers and went outside to play
their hunting game—one was the hunter, the other was the deer,
who, when shot with a stick, would have to collapse on the ground,
legs and arms sprawled, tongue sticking out, eyes rolling—
I would tell them, "I don't want to hear it unless there's blood."

The doctor asks me to scoot down and spread my legs. Wider.
"You're going to feel something cold," he says, inserting the wand.
I try to focus on the flowers blooming in the creases
of my elbows. (The nurse couldn't find a good vein.)

On the screen: no tangled, fisted orb.
No inexplicable mass. Just my empty sac, cloud-swept.
"Cloud-swept" is my attempt at lyric expression.
I wanted this poem to be shorter, snappier, but I can't help it.
In workshop the poet E once told me I tend toward the discursive.
"We all have our tendencies," she said. The key is to temper
those impulses like the Greeks did with tragedy.
It's the old tension between the Apollonian and the Dionysian.
Order versus chaos—the balance between them,
what to leave in, what you can live without.

~

Postmortem Say

Could say crimsoned limbs
and blood moon glass shatter, say
he was chrome smoke, the night
diamond-flecked, say the cause
was exsanguination due to blunt
force trauma from a wreck,
say too many contributing
factors to list. Or say the truth,
which is to say: it was dark,
we never saw each other,
say by the time we did,
it was already too late,
the loss total.

ABOUT THE AUTHOR

Amanda Newell is the author of *I Will Pass Even to Acheron*, a 2021 winner of the Rattle Chapbook Prize, and *Fractured Light* (Broadkill River Press), winner of the 2010 Dogfish Head Poetry Prize. Her poems have appeared in *Bellevue Literary Review*, *Cimarron Review*, *Gargoyle*, *Rattle*, *Scoundrel Time*, and elsewhere. A graduate of The MFA Program for Writers at Warren Wilson College, she has received scholarships from the Bread Loaf Writers' Conference and The Frost Place as well as a fellowship from the Virginia Center for the Creative Arts. She is an associate editor at *Plume*.

www.ingramcontent.com/pod-product-compliance
Lightning Source LLC
Chambersburg PA
CBHW031935080426
42734CB00007B/695